Jeanne —
 Please share this with Shari after you read it. She was supposed to get one, but I goofed on the order.
   B.S.

Mop Bucket Meditations

Published by Mar-Bear Publishing
606 Mary Hughes Drive
Houma, Louisiana 70363

Limited First Edition
Copyright © 2005 by Marion Haines Duplantis

All rights reserved, including the right to reproduce, store or transmit this book or any portion thereof in any form whatsoever without prior written permission of the author.

Excerpts from the *New American Bible with Revised New Testament and Psalms* Copyright © 1991, 1986, 1970 Confraternity of Christian Doctrine, Inc., Washington, DC. Used with permission. All rights reserved. No portion of the *New American Bible* may be reprinted without permission in writing from the copyright holder.

For information or to order copies of this book, contact:
  Mar-Bear Publishing
  985-872-3897

ISBN: 0-9725452-1-2

Contents in this work are meant to be inspirational and no slights of people or places are intentional. Any similarities to persons living or dead is purely coincidental.

Page layout by JANLO Services Publishing
Editing by CAL's Concepts
Illustrations by Claudine Claudet Boquet
Published in the United States of America
Printed in China

Dedication

I once read that "children are the anchors that hold a mother to life." My five children, Phyllis, Michelle, Derel, Brendan and Joel have certainly been those anchors. They have provided me with fun and laughter. I have shed many tears for them as well. Without them, however, I would have no stories to tell. My life would have been an empty canvas. Now I am blessed with grandchildren: Aaron, Seth, Stephanie, Danielle, Sydney, Shaylyn, Quinn, Annelise and my great grand-daughter, Allie. God certainly loves me and I know it. I dedicate this book to all of you. Know, without a shadow of a doubt, how much I truly love you. I am grateful for the love you have given to me through the years. You have all made me extremely proud and I am honored to be your mother and grandmother!

I hope that the prayers and meditations within this book will help other mothers who are struggling with life, in general. Enjoy your families! Do a lot of laughing with your children. Learn to laugh at yourself too!

Table of Contents

Author's Note	1
Wrapping Paper	3
Outlets	5
Lights Out	7
Rainbows	9
Candles	11
Nutshells	13
Bathroom Tile	15
Breadcrumbs	17
Baking	19
Dirty Drinking Glasses	21
Muffins	23
Junk Drawers	25
Dust	27
Unmatched Socks	29
Crooked Fork	31
Motherhood	33
Pretty Dishes	35
Spring Cleaning	37
About The Author	39

Author's Note

    As I go about my everyday activities of a wife and mother, I am sometimes overwhelmed with the responsibilities that seem to pull at me from all directions. At times, I become discouraged and begin to meditate on my trying circumstances. In my human weakness I blame myself or others for my situation. In the midst of my confusion, disappointment, anger, resentment, jealousy and longing I call out to the Lord. I literally have conversations with Him in my mind. Deep inside my heart I hear Him respond in a loving manner with words of encouragement. Even as He gently disciplines me, I know that He desires to mold character in me for His good pleasure.

    In these intimate moments of reflection and conversation I have taken time to write what is on my heart. The compilation of these resulted in Mop Bucket Meditations. It is my desire that this book will comfort, inspire and encourage you as you journey through the difficult seasons of life. I sincerely hope that God's encouraging words found in this book help you in your search for love of yourself and others; acceptance of life's daily lessons; and spiritual growth.

Wrapping Paper

It seems like such a waste. Packages piled so high, gaily dressed in all of their splendor, soon to be ripped apart by the anxious recipient. And there the costly paper lies, crumpled on the floor to be disposed of in the trash.

"God, am I like that? Do I place so much emphasis on the outer wrap that will certainly be disposed of some day that I forget the important part - the GIFT of life within me? Or, do I use the outer covering to hide my insecurities from others?"

"Rip away my vanity, God. Tear away at my pride until only the gift of Your love and life are exposed to the world."

-Psalm 119:37
Avert my eyes from what is worthless;
  by your way give me life.

Outlets

It's hard to imagine all of the power that lies within the outlets in these walls. There's enough to turn on a TV, a vacuum cleaner, a microwave and hundreds of other items at the same time. Yet, that power is of no use to me unless something is plugged into it.

I heard God say to me, "My Holy Spirit is like that outlet…waiting for anyone who desires, to plug into the power. With that power, comes change. With that power, there is the ability to accomplish many things that could never have been done before in your spiritual walk with Me."

-Luke 10:19
Behold, I have given you power 'to tread upon serpents' and scorpions and upon the full force of the enemy and nothing will harm you.

-Acts 1:8
But you will receive power when the holy Spirit comes upon you, and you will be my witnesses in Jerusalem, throughout Judea and Samaria, and to the ends of the earth.

Lights Out

I had just started peeling potatoes for dinner when the electricity went out in the neighborhood. Needing to see better, I pulled up the shades, and then opened the windows to let the cool breezes blow through the house.

In my day-to-day hustle and bustle, I forgot to listen to the sounds of nature's world. It was wonderful just to hear the sound of the knife peeling the potatoes, my breath, the birds and crickets. Where had they been all this time? Rather, where had I been? Lately I have looked at the world only through the windows, but not opened those windows to embrace the real world on the other side. Yes, I saw it and it was beautiful! But, I was missing so much by not smelling, touching and living it.

-Psalm 9:1-3
I will praise you, LORD, with all my heart;
    I will declare all your wondrous deeds.
I will delight and rejoice in you;
    I will sing hymns to your name, Most
        High

Rainbows

Looking out of my kitchen window, a beautiful rainbow appeared. "Funny," I thought, "It's raining in the front yard and in the back yard there's this gorgeous rainbow."

That's how so many people look at life. Even though it's storming on one side, they fail to look at the good side, the side of promise. The Lord says to remember His promises. They'll bring you through all those storms in your life.

2 Peter 3:9
The Lord does not delay his promise, as some regard "delay," but he is patient with you, not wishing that any should perish but that all should come to repentance.

Candles

The last time the lights went out, I promised myself that I'd remember where I put the pack of candles. Yet, here I sit in the darkness, again. When will I ever learn to put them in a convenient place? I need them to light the way around the house. Tonight, I promise to put the candles where I can find them easily in the dark.

I heard the Lord say to me, "I've placed you, like a candle, to lighten the world where you live. Only you somehow remained hidden, unseen just when I needed you the most to light another's path. When your light is placed with others, the world will no longer be shrouded in darkness, but filled with the light of My glory."

-Matthew 5:14-16
You are the light of the world. A city set on a mountain cannot be hidden. Nor do they light a lamp and then put it under a bushel basket; it is set on a lampstand, where it gives light to all in the house. Just so, your light must shine before others, that they may see your good deeds and glorify your heavenly Father.

Nutshells

I often wonder who the first person was to taste a nut. Looking at it from the outside certainly wouldn't cause a person's mouth to water. Who was the tenacious soul who broke through the nutshell and gave the nut a chance to prove its worth?

"Lord, I thank you for the first person who cracked my shell and discovered my worth. I know that You always knew it was there. Somehow though, it's comforting to know that others can love me as I am. With all of my outer shell ripped away, I stand exposed and vulnerable before them. They don't cast me aside, but daily learn to appreciate the goodness that is within me."

-Proverbs 17:17
He who is a friend is always a friend,
   and a brother is born for the time of
        stress.

Bathroom Tile

"Why is it, God, when I visit someone else's home, her tile sparkles and shines? Mine never are what I want them to be."

In my heart I felt the Lord say, "Every day, she probably wipes down the walls to keep them clean. It must be done daily to keep them spotless. Your life can be made spotless like these walls, by DAILY wiping down the walls of your mind. Every night before going to bed, remove the scum which has formed through your day-to-day activities. The scum of gossip, unforgiveness, worry and whatever else would keep you from shining!"

Isaiah 60:1
Rise up in splendor! Your light has come,
*   the glory of the Lord shines upon you.*

Bread Crumbs

"Why do loaves of bread have crusts?" I wondered. A person can accumulate only so many bags of crusts and the family doesn't care for bread pudding every day.

Gathering them in a bowl, I crumbled them up and proceeded out of the back door to throw them to the many birds that were flying around.

I washed the dishes quietly so as not to disturb the gathering for the feast of crumbs. Birds of all sizes and colors darted back and forth, taking the choicest morsels to their young.

All of a sudden, one big black bird swooped down, spread his wings and puffed up his chest as if to say, "These are my crumbs and mine only. I'm the sole possessor of them, get out of my way."

"God, You are the giver of all gifts. You give them out freely to be used by all. Forgive me if I ever lord over Your gifts and act as if I am the sole possessor of them all. Teach me to share with others the gifts that you've given me."

-1 Corinthians 12:4-7
There are different kinds of spiritual gifts but the same spirit; there are different forms of service but the same Lord; there are different workings but the same God who produces all of them in everyone. To each individual the manifestation of the Spirit is given for some benefit.

Baking

No wonder it's flat and tasteless. The recipe called for three eggs and I added only two because I would need the other egg later. And, it's way too sweet. That extra cup of sugar wasn't called for in the recipe book, but I like things sweet. The powdered coffee creamer wasn't such a good idea as a substitute for whipping cream either. Oh, well, I guess I'm just not a good cook.

I felt God answer, "Do you use my recipe book for life the same way as you cook? In My book, I have directions for every area of your life. But, there are no shortcuts, no substitutions or additions. The directions in My book are explicit, step-by-step, simple ways to obtain a perfect product…YOU!

Psalm 138:8
The LORD is with me to the end.
    LORD, your love endures forever.
    Never forsake the work of your hands!

Dirty Drinking Glasses

When I see a fault in someone, help me to think of it as a dirty drinking glass.

Lord, I see the junk in someone's life and it bothers me to see the entire residue clinging to that person.

God said to me, "Your job is only to lift those people up to the springs of living water. My water will saturate and cleanse the crustiness of their life and leave them sparkling. Your ONLY job is to lift them up to Me, the living, cleansing water of life."

-Psalm 36: 9-10
We feast on the rich food of your house;
    from your delightful stream you give us
        drink.
For with you is the fountain of life,
    and in your light we see light.

Muffins

    I mixed the batter quickly and gave the bowl to my friend, Ginger, to spoon into the tins. Confessing earlier that she felt insecure with her baking skills, I praised her for her ability to spoon the dough into the tins so neatly. I then made my dough and spooned the batter into the tins.

    With baking time completed, it was the moment of truth. Mine were flat and hers were beautiful. Pride and insecurity rose up within me. "What will everyone think of my flat, hard muffins? I am the good cook who bakes all of the time."

    "Throw them all away," I thought. I argued with myself, "No, it's 1:30 in the morning and too late to bake more."

    The next morning before the women's meeting I reluctantly placed Ginger's muffins next to mine and walked into the meeting. Fluffy, puffy muffins adorned the tables. Inadequacy crept into my spirit.

    The other ladies adjourned to a separate room and left Ginger and me with the secretary. The secretary immediately took the smallest muffin from our tray and ate it. Then she ate another one.

"Isn't that just like you, God, to let me know that you even care about my miserable little muffins? You used another person to show me that no matter what small, inadequate thing I do for You, that You notice. It's never too small or inadequate to You."

-Psalm 103:11
As the heavens tower over the earth,
    so God's love towers over the faithful.

Junk Drawers

One of these days, I'm going to clean them out. Every day, I stuff something into them, especially when company is driving up and I need to make a quick, clean sweep of the house. I wouldn't dare let anyone see all of the trash that I've jammed into that small space, but I know it's there. I've just got to set it in order. . . . tomorrow…or maybe next week…or next year.

My heart felt God say, "You have a part of your life that is like that. Every day you say, 'I've got to get control of that area,' but then, you stuff it back tightly so no one will see or know. It won't go away, it will always be there, nagging at you until it is cleaned out and put in proper order."

-Psalm 139:7-8, 16
Where can I hide from your spirit?
    From your presence, where can I flee?
If I ascend to the heavens, you are there;
    if I lie down in Sheol, you are there
        too.

Your eyes foresaw my actions;
    in your book all are written down;
    my days were shaped, before one came
        to be.

Dust

Where does it all come from? Every day it appears from nowhere; making its silent appearance, but loudly screaming at me the moment company appears at the door.

I felt God say, "That's how sin comes in, silently, steadily, until it covers the whole being. You don't seem to notice it because it's a pang of jealousy here; a bit of greed there; a secret lust somewhere else; and a touch of pride everywhere in between. Little by little and hour by hour sin takes over, covering the beauty that is beneath it."

"Dust me Lord, shine me, and polish me. I want all traces of sin to be wiped away so others may see your face, reflecting off of my very being."

-Psalm 51:9, 12
Cleanse me with hyssop, that I may be
      pure;
  wash me, make me whiter than snow.

A clean heart create for me, God;
    renew in me a steadfast spirit.

Unmatched Socks

There must be a lesson somewhere in these unmatched socks, Lord. Either the machine eats them or my teenage sons have them as snacks.

Everywhere in the world, there are people who feel like they don't match. They don't fit in with all the others. Always, it seems, they are set aside for the ones who fit in. Day by day, other mismatches are piled on top of them until finally they are lost in a sea of sizes, colors and shapes.

"Help me to pray daily for those who don't fit, God. I know how it feels when people look you over and cast you aside because you're not the same as others. Yes, Lord, I forgive those who have done this to me. And if I have done this to anyone, please forgive me."

-1 Corinthians 12:19-20, 26
If they were all one part, where would the body be? But as it is, there are many parts, yet one body...
If [one] part suffers, all the parts suffer with it; if one part is honored, all the parts share its joy.

Crooked Fork

I really wanted to impress her today, God. The table was ready and the food cooked to perfection. I had hoped to surely please her this time. But, just as she removed the fork from her mouth, I noticed it. I had given her the fork with the crooked tines! It's funny now, but yesterday it wasn't. Miss Perfection had become unperfected in a hurry.

Forgive me, God, when I try so hard to impress others when in reality, it is only You I need to impress. Help me laugh at myself when I am being humbled.

-1Peter 5:5-6
Likewise, you younger members, be subject to the presbyters.
And all of you, clothe yourselves with humility
in your dealings with one another, for:

   "God opposes the proud
      but bestows favor on the humble."

So humble yourselves under the mighty hand
of God, that he may exalt you in due time.

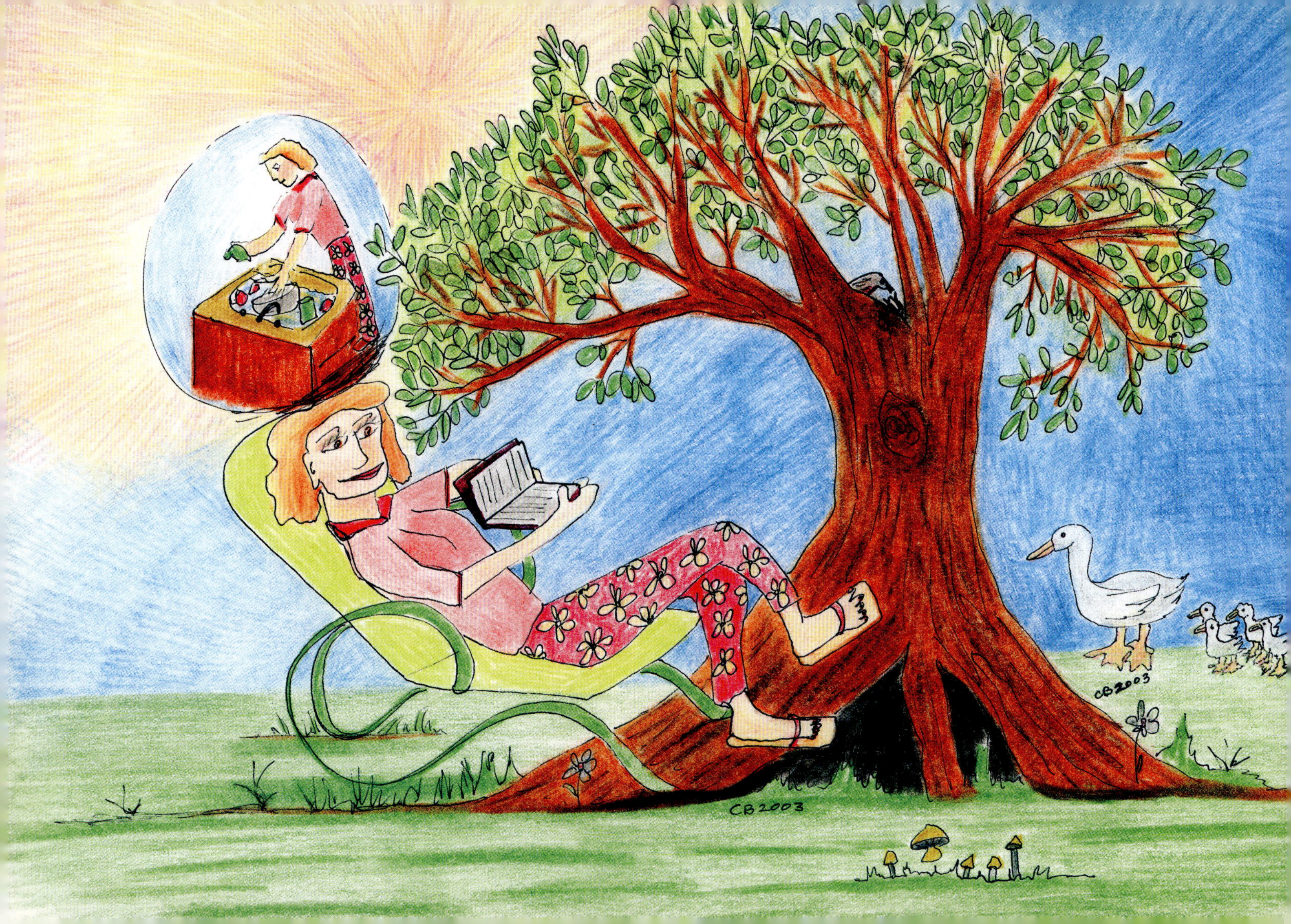
CB2003
CB2003

Motherhood

"This job of motherhood is not all it's cracked up to be. Sometimes I don't know how much more I can take. I'm being pulled in so many directions by so many people. It's so much easier being saintly by lounging under a tree and reading God's word or bowing reverently in church. I wonder why God speaks to me so loudly when I'm raising my hands at a prayer meeting."

God answered me, "I'm speaking to you all day long as you put the wash in the machine; or, as you watch the soup bubbling in the pot. I have a lesson for you to learn in everything you do while you're mothering. Be content. Start seeking the simple lessons that I am teaching you right in your home, amid the pots and pans. Many, many saints were made amid mountains of dirty clothes and dishes. You can be one too!"

-1 Corinthians 1:27
Rather, God chose the foolish of the world to shame the wise, and God chose the weak of the world to shame the strong.

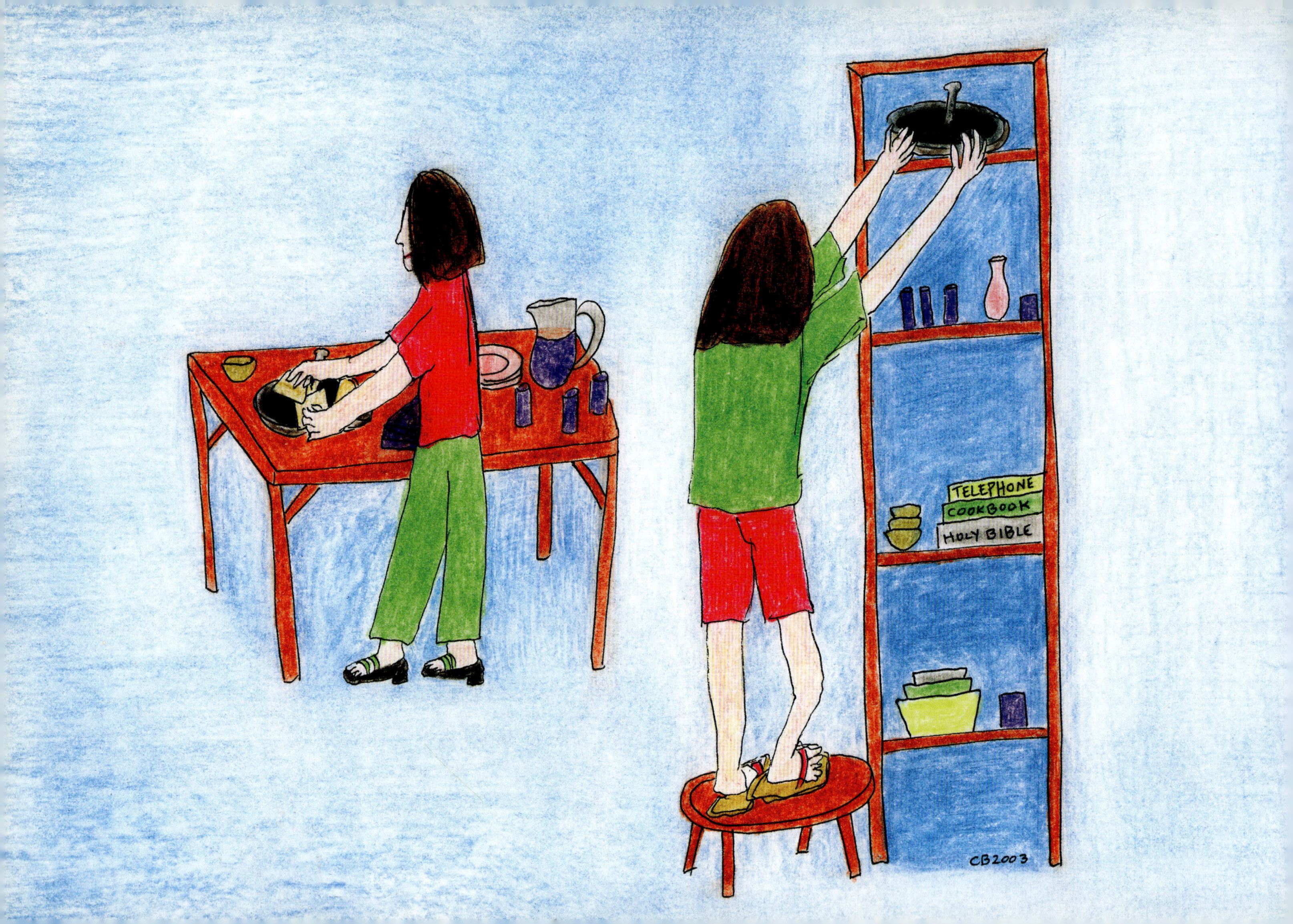
TELEPHONE
COOKBOOK
HOLY BIBLE
CB2003

Pretty Dishes

I used Grandma's black onyx sandwich plate for every occasion that came up in the family. I'd proudly place it outside on the card table for the children's parties or pile freshly made sandwiches on it for holiday gatherings. It was a functional dish and an everyday part of my life. But, then I found out that it was very valuable and set it out to view. Now, there it sits as pretty as ever and as useful as ever, but just collecting dust.

God whispered to me, "Through the years people have done the exact same thing to My word, the Bible! It used to be an everyday, functional part of their lives. Now, it's a decoration. Like your pretty plate, it's collecting dust and not being used at all for the purposes for which it was intended."

-Psalm 119:105
Your word is a lamp for my feet,
    a light for my path.

-Proverbs 4:4
He taught me, and said to me:
    "Let your heart hold fast my words:
    keep my commands, that you may live!"

HATE
JEALOUSY
PREJUDICE
ENVY
BAD BEHAVIOR
PAIN
INSECURITY
FEAR
OVER WORK
CB2003

Spring Cleaning

It's that time of the year, again! It's the time when everything needs to be turned upside down and inside out, examined, explored, fixed, thrown away, packed up, mended or passed on to someone else.

God instructed my heart, "This year, I'd like to do a major spring cleaning on you. We'll start from the attic of your mind and end at the basement of your toes. You may get tired and even angry along the way, but always keep in mind the end results of a sparkling clean home for Me.

We won't try to do it all in one day. If we do that, it won't be as thorough a cleaning. It's best to take our time, one room at a time. Don't think about any other room while we're cleaning. When you do that, we can't be as effective in the room we're working on at the moment. Think of only one room at a time and then it won't overwhelm you.

I plan to stay with you the entire time we're cleaning. I'll help you every step of the way. Having a special close friend assist during spring cleaning is often helpful. The reason that I want to start in the attic of your mind is because so many of your past failings and hurts are stored there. These are of no use to you anymore. They take up entirely too much space. This is space that could be used for more productive thoughts. You'll need a big garbage can for the attic, because through the years you've collected memories and thoughts that should not be stored anymore. These are like storing dangerous combustible material in a real attic. They can ignite the whole area in a flame that is unquenchable.

Old attitudes need to be discarded, too. You must empty your mind of any prejudice, jealousy, envy, or hate. Throw away any other old attitude that keeps you from loving! No need to have these boxes of bad behavior laying around taking up valuable space. We're almost finished here. Let's sweep out any remembrances of the past now and leave it clean and empty. It is to be filled only with 'whatsoever is pure and holy'. Think on these things.

Your arms are next. Have they embraced all of the ones I've told you to embrace? Have they reached out to the widow, orphan, prisoner, those held captive, the unloved and the unlovable? I've asked you to love them all; not just say that you love them. Do something physical to show them. Embrace them; hold them close to your heart, like I do.

continued on next page

Your heart is like the kitchen area that needs daily attention. Like the attic, you've stored many, many people's lives and secrets in your heart. This is good, but can also be a hindrance if too many things are stored. Clean out the crevices of your heart. The areas where you've been scarred are there too. I'll help repair those scars. They've been there so long. It may take some time, but I promise that when I finish with your heart, it will be like new.

I know that you must be getting tired. We're almost through. We just have the windows and basement left.

Your eyes are like the windows. I want them to shine at all times. They are often so clouded by the cares of the day, that My light can't shine out. Keep them shining at all times so that others may know that I live in your house too.

Let's go down to the basement now. It is sort of like your day-to-day life. Everything is overstuffed and disorganized at times. This room will take a while but that's why I am here."

About The Author

Marion Haines Duplantis was introduced to music ministry at an early age. Her mother, Hazel Nary Haines, served as the organist for several different churches, both Catholic and Protestant, resulting in the author's exposure to many different religions and all kinds of beautiful music. As a result of this, she totally immersed herself in music by singing in the school girls' quartet, the choir and an octet. Marion performed in several musical productions and was selected to sing at several Music Educators National Conferences as well as the Hollywood Bowl during her high school years.

A graduate of Pacific High School in San Bernardino, California, she moved to Houma, Louisiana, at the age of eighteen, married Camille C. Duplantis, III at the age of nineteen, and remained active in music by singing in Little Theatre productions and church choirs. Blessed with five children, Duplantis was kept very busy over the years doing what she calls "mothering duties."

Marion said, "I led a local music ministry for over ten years and sang with Kerry Bueche Ministries for several years. During this time I released a tape of original songs I felt the Lord had given me called *Jesus is the Answer*. For several years, I lead a prayer group for troubled teens struggling with drugs and other problems. I was active in *Women's Aglow* for many years, played the guitar and sang on Bishop Boudreaux's weekly television show for several years and I am still active in *Magnificat*, a wonderful ministry for women."

Marion added, "My writing career began with my writing of a skit to be used in the Cleanest City Contest, called "*Auntie Litter*," for which we won the state award. After the play had been presented in every school in the parish, I sold the play to several other Louisiana cities. Before this, I had only written poetry.

When my grandson, Aaron, was in fourth grade, I wrote a story about a little pumpkin who wanted to be someone special. My first book, "*The Little Pumpkin*", was published in 2002. I have several other books already written that will follow *Mop Bucket Meditations*."

Marion added, "My illustrator, Claudine Boquet, has always enjoyed being creative, so it was only natural for her to have taken an interest in art studies at Nicholls State University. This marks the first time her work is published."